IN PRAISE
OF LEARNING

Into Our Third Century Series

The Church in a Changing Society, William E. Ramsden
Images of the Future, Alan K. Waltz
In Praise of Learning, Donald B. Rogers
Women, Change, and the Church, Nancy J. Van Scoyoc
Shaping the Congregation, Robert L. Wilson
Ministries Through Non-Parish Institutions, William E. Ramsden
Sources and Shapes of Power,
  John R. Sherwood and John C. Wagner

IN PRAISE
OF LEARNING

DONALD B. ROGERS

Ezra Earl Jones, Editor

ABINGDON   Nashville

IN PRAISE OF LEARNING

Library of Congress Cataloging in Publication Data

ROGERS, DONALD B 1931-
    In praise of learning.
    1. Christian education—Philosophy. 2. Learning. I. Title.
BV1464.R6   207   79-26829

ISBN 0-687-18910-1

MANUFACTURED BY THE PARTHENON PRESS AT
NASHVILLE, TENNESSEE, UNITED STATES OF AMERICA

Contents

FOREWORD 7

ACKNOWLEDGMENTS 11

CHAPTER ONE
Introduction 13

CHAPTER TWO
Themes of Learning Styles 17

CHAPTER THREE
To Teachers 24

CHAPTER FOUR
To Learners 31

CHAPTER FIVE
To Parents and Grandparents 37

CHAPTER SIX
To Pastors, Educators, and Other Leaders 46

CHAPTER SEVEN
To Children 54

CHAPTER EIGHT
On Listening 59

Foreword

In 1984 United Methodism will observe the two-hundredth anniversary of the Christmas Conference of 1784—the date most often regarded as the beginning of the Methodist movement in the United States. We shall pause to remember how the Wesleyan vision of holy love and active piety spread like an unquenchable flame as the United States expanded from coast to coast; how people of all races, cultures, and classes rallied to a gospel offering salvation and demanding good works as the fruit of Christian faith in God.

But we shall do more. Our bicentennial is also a time to soberly anticipate the future, to take stock of ourselves as we move into our third century. Our inheritance is rich in faith and works. It nourishes us, but our tasks are now and tomorrow. The United Methodist Church is large (9.7 million members in the United States), still highly visible and active, but some indicators of our future prospects are disturbing. We shall reflect on and discuss these concerns as United Methodists until we once again catch a vision of ministry and service that is worthy of our past, builds upon our present, and thrusts us again into the mainstream of human life with the message of God's redeeming love.

You, a United Methodist lay member or pastor, and your congregation have a vital role in both the celebration and the search. It is the people in the pews

and pulpits of United Methodism who must reestablish
our identity and purpose through discussion of who we
are as United Methodists, what we wish to accomplish,
and how we pursue our goals in the years ahead.

A Research Design for United Methodism as It Enters
Its Third Century, initiated by the General Council on
Ministries with the encouragement of the Council of
Bishops, is intended to support your efforts. It is an
extensive study of selected issues of fundamental
ministry and organizational concern to the denomina-
tion and a study of the environment in which United
Methodism in the United States serves. Over a four-year
period beginning in 1980, eighteen separate volumes are
being released for your use. The present book, *In Praise
of Learning*, is the third volume in the series and the first
one to deal with a specific issue or aspect of the church's
life. The initial books in this series, *The United Methodist
Church in a Changing Society* and *Images of the Future*, were
released earlier this year. Those volumes provide basic
information and background for this and later volumes.
Subsequent volumes will deal with the present realities
and future form, content, and challenges of outreach
ministry (mission, evangelism, and social witness); social
movements and issues; church leadership and management; nonparish institutions (for example, colleges,
hospitals, homes, and community centers); local
churches as community institutions; women in church
and society; ecumenical relationships; ethnic minority
constituencies; understanding faith (the role of theology); professional ministry; general agencies; financial
support; and polity (the philosophy and form of church
government and the organization).

The General Council on Ministries commends to you
now this volume by Donald Rogers. Basing his research

on scores of interviews with United Methodists of diverse ages and relationship to the church, Dr. Rogers has focused on a much-neglected aspect of Christian education—namely, what the church teaches by all that it is and does. You can read this book in an evening, but we predict that your fascination with the insights it offers will continue much longer. Share your reflections within your own congregation, with other Christians, and with district, conference, and general church leaders. Your response and inquiries will also be welcomed by the members and staff of the council.

Norman E. Dewire
General Secretary

Ezra Earl Jones
Editor

The General Council on Ministries
601 West Riverview Avenue
Dayton, Ohio 45406

April, 1980

Acknowledgments

Many people have helped in the process that led to this book. I am particularly grateful to the people who shared of themselves in the interviews and to those in the churches who helped arrange the schedules. Anonymity was a part of the contract we made with those people, so my expression of appreciation must be general. It is nonetheless a deep and genuine word of thanks.

Interviews were conducted and other chores handled by Marilyn Benson, Kathy Ferris, Phyllis May, Connie Rogers, Linda Shaw, and Cean Wilson. They helped greatly. The arduous task of turning the taped interviews into typed manuscripts was performed with great dedication by Nancy Barnett. My thanks to them all.

All along the way I had the privilege of being in conversation with members of the advisory panel for this project, consisting of Jim Anderson, Episcopal diocese of Washington, D.C.; Edith M. Goodwin, the General Council on Ministries; Howard Ham, the Board of Discipleship; David Kidd, United Methodist pastor in Flint, Michigan; and Phyllis May, Christian educator. Ezra Earl Jones of the General Council on Ministries served as the convener of that group as well as executive director of the project. He provided encouragement and guidance in a gracious manner. I am deeply indebted to the panel for their assistance.

Members of the faculty and staff of United Theological Seminary (Dayton) provided the kind of support and interest that makes such a task as this all the more exciting.

CHAPTER 1

Introduction

The Source of This Book

One question has been the focal point of the process leading to this book: How do people learn? That question was directed to people in churches scattered among urban, suburban, small-town, and rural America. In hour-long interviews, people answered that question, taking many directions and touching many factors.

If education is based on learning, and if the learning that is critical can be described by the learners, then the future of education in the church can have as a part of its planning both a process and some general indicators of what should be our next step. We have conducted these interviews with the bias that learning is natural and normal and is, in fact, going on. We will not have a sufficiently full picture of learning if we restrict our exploration to the response people make to formal programs of instruction. It is that fuller picture, painted by the learner and noted by the attentive listener, that we have sought.

In each church setting, the interviews were conducted with pastors, experienced church-school teachers, parents, fourth-grade children, inactive church members, lay and/or professional religious educators, and teen-agers. The interviews were taped, transcribed, and reviewed by the advisory panel of professional educators.

The review process led to the identification of important themes that appeared in the descriptions, using repetition and centrality as the criteria. Those themes have become the basic threads of this book. Around them we have constructed the statements that comprise the sections.

The Objectives of the Book

The major objective of the book is to encourage persons in the church to take the time to listen carefully to the learners with whom they work. What is stated in the book is not intended to be prescriptive. Rather, by reading about these interviews and the themes and seeing how one person speculates on their significance, it is hoped that many others will explore their own settings, find their own themes, and draw their own conclusions.

A secondary objective is to elevate the importance as well as the complexity of learner behavior. How people learn is seen to be of fundamental importance in education decision-making and teaching. While learning theory, with its base in psychology, is of use in answering this question, the pattern of learner behavior is more complex than learning theory is intended to comprehend.

Learning is a pattern of behavior as well as a process of the mind. It involves to whom one listens, what one reads, how one views the teacher, as well as how much insight and reinforcement one gains. Learning is a pattern of habits and preferences and motivation as well as memorization and model imitation.

We have realized in the gasoline crisis that conservation can take place if advice can be directed to the driving patterns of automobile users. While a survey that shows the ebb and flow of gas consumption, as related to miles driven, is of great usefulness, the little quirks and eccentricities of individual drivers must also be known. Further still, we must come to see the use of the automobile from the perspective of the drivers if we are to meet the problems at the place of consumption and possible conservation.

A similar rationale has motivated the interviewing on which this book is based. We have projected that it is of critical importance to see the learning that goes on in and around the church from the *point of view of the learners*. We have avoided as much as possible methods that tend to obscure the unique style of each learner. In the text that follows, you will find generalizations, but it is hoped that the original intent to focus on the unique individual will not be lost. It is for that reason that we encourage you to do your own on-site listening.

It is the richness of variation among learners that is both the problem and the promise of making decisions about education in the church. We must face the variations among people as learners and respond to their individuality of style, while at the same time attempting to make decisions that will serve groups of people. This tension between individuality and group programming will lead us to relevant education *if* we will take the time to listen to learners as they describe their styles and *if* we will take those descriptions seriously.

How to Read This Book

The book begins with an exposition of the identifiable themes from the interview research. Sections addressed to five specific audiences follow. The book concludes with a section on listening. We suggest that you read the first section on themes, the section that most centrally

includes you, and the last section on listening. Then we
invite you, if inclined, to read sections that are addressed
to others.

We suggest you read with the hope of finding yourself
described in part, but not fully. Read with these questions
in your mind: How am I the same and yet different in my
learning style? How do the learners I work with fit this
pattern? As you become conscious of your style and that
of others in your context, your sensitivity to learners is
increased.

What to Do After Reading the Book

Our fondest hope will be fulfilled if those who read the
book then will engage in their own research. One form of
that research can be to sit down with one person and
invite that person to describe as fully as possible his or her
learning process.

Others may conduct an introspective research project
by putting down for themselves a description of their
own learning style. For many people the process of
learning is so much a part of their lives that they are not
really very conscious of it.

Some may find the time and see the importance of
talking to a larger group of people, a selected and
perhaps representative cross section of the learners they
find in and around the formal and intentional learning
experiences of their church.

If your experience is like ours, you will find yourself
rediscovering the obvious far more often than coming
across the brand new and unknown. But you will also
find that the "obvious" is given new vitality and will
become a firm new base for decisions about what to do in
the teaching/learning ministry of the church.

CHAPTER 2

Themes of Learning Style

We listened. We listened to people in The United Methodist Church as they told us about the ways they learn. Women and men, adults and children, teachers and teen-agers, pastors and educators, blacks and whites and people of other races.

We listened to the great variety of styles and common themes as the open conversations filled the hour. People talked about this topic even though it was a puzzling issue. They talked with a sincerity and energy and openness that surprised us. They talked with a hunger to be heard. One woman said: "I'd like to be in a class that maybe I could say something that somebody would listen to. They don't really seem to be too interested in what I have to say."

That hunger to be heard is one of the things we learned about their learning. They commented too frequently for chance about how much they had learned by talking to us. A teen-ager commented, "This interview may be another way of God trying to remind me that he's still around and he still wants me."

And an inactive man said: "You see, it's very seldom that you get an opportunity to sit down and talk about this sort of thing. . . . But I think as a result of this I feel that probably, maybe not the very next time that you see me, but I think I'm going to do some serious thinking about joining a church."

These people who talked to us said that the church can do something very valuable for learners by providing them with the time and space and a person to listen to what they have to say. *Listening* is one of the major themes to be addressed in this book.

As we listened we found ourselves discovering the obvious. It is not news to learn that for many of those we listened to, *caring persons* have been a major part of their most significant times of learning. An adult recalled: "It's the Sunday school teacher who takes the time to care with children. So often I have forgotten so many of the things that I learned, but I never forgot the teachers that cared."

What was fresh about this well-known facet of learning was the quiet emotional intensity that surrounded the memories of those caring persons. There was a way in which something that was true had stronger verification—a way in which the obvious became even clearer.

Caring persons, who were in the lives of our learners long enough and/or deeply enough for that care to become known and trusted, became sources of knowledge. They became models of truth; they became sources of information; they provided wisdom. The learners learned because of that caring relationship. Hearing learners describe these real people had a strong impact.

Wisdom from wise people was another theme in what we heard. A surprising number of times our learners would describe a person, a grandparent or a neighbor or a Sunday school teacher, and tell us some bit of wisdom they learned from that person and still remembered as a key to life.

Other times it was a memory of a longer relationship to a wise person. A pastor recalled:

One of the real reasons that I'm in the ministry is that when I was a teen-ager in high school, my Sunday school teacher—she was not brilliantly educated but she really understood life—this lady gave us so much through the high school years.

We noticed that those bits of wisdom sometimes were very small capsules of truth to the point of being trite.

He never puts more on you than you can bear.

The Bible says that God takes care of babies and fools.

The normal part of your life will be back.

God gives you the strength for the day.

In all thy ways acknowledge him and he shall direct your paths—that's one you can say over and over every day.

As we mused over this, one of us suggested that those sayings were more important as tags for whole relationships than as little lessons. The sayings were ways of recalling those people and the times of being with them. The church can help people learn by encouraging wise people to share themselves, particularly with children.

We heard our learners talk time and again about the lasting influence of learning that took place when they were young children:

It's amazing what you can use that you learned when you were in second and third grade. I always felt like I really didn't know much. I mean I feel like I don't know very much about the Bible, but when I started preparing I found that I knew more than I thought.

You already know this, too, as a dependable generality. What you may find as interesting as we did is that people can and will describe moments in that span of life with loving care.

It is not clear when this next thematic pattern begins in
the learning process, but the motivation for learning in
many adults is a rather ordinary and simple desire to live
their daily lives in a Christian manner. People learn in
order to handle the daily routine of life. They also learn
in order to resolve the focused crisis moments. Sometimes they learn out of simple curiosity, but learning for
learning's sake takes a back seat to learning for living's
sake.

Here is one "confession" about motivation for learning:

> I don't tend to concentrate on something unless I see a need in
> myself for doing it. Is there an empty spot that needs to be
> filled? . . . I'm the one who sounds crassly selfish, what's in it for
> me? But I know why I attended those seminars and worked on
> it—boy, as hard as I have ever worked—because I could see right
> away that they were going to make some changes for me that I just
> had to have or I wouldn't have survived.

Perhaps it is the way in which the daily life is so
involving that puts it at the front among motivation
patterns. People told us how important it was to them to
be involved in order to learn. For some this took the form
of involvement in classroom activity. For many it was the
job they were asked to do in the church or community
that provoked their learning. Children described choirs
and worship roles and plays and concerts as bright
moments of learning. Looking back from a distance of
many years an adult reflected,

> "I enjoy the memories of Children's Day, when we were little, when
> we used to go and say a piece."

The learners we listened to seemed to be *ad hoc*
utilitarians. They learned what they needed to know in

order to do something. We did not hear many people describe a steady progression in learning. The patterns were more spasmodic and, frankly, erratic. This pattern may be somewhat upsetting to those who have to plan education for others, but it is characteristic of learners.

The learners we listened to were not unhappy about their learning patterns or about their knowledge. Oh yes, many of them "guessed they could always learn some more about the Bible," but they were not, for the most part, disappointed with themselves or the church as far as teaching and learning goes.

When you listen you may hear a different story, but even the inactive people who talked to us were not carrying a grudge about the church's teaching ministry. In what struck us as somewhat childlike, adults learned from the feeling of the atmosphere and aroma of the climate. Learners are shaped and molded more often than they are taught.

Another way to say what is described in the preceding paragraphs is that learners approach this task of learning in a nontechnical and nontechnological mind set. We began to speculate that a good part of the nostalgia we heard was based on an unarticulated desire to simplify teaching and learning. Education may be in an awkward stage of development: knowing too much about learning and development patterns and other technical insights just to teach; and knowing too little about the significance of those insights to go beyond them with a renewed and more profound simplicity.

We did not find learners coming to the education process with high expectations that they would be changed, especially not radically changed. That may present something of a challenge too, since our culture places a heavy change agenda on the education process. We teach, some say, in order to change people and change society. I am rather confident I have a lot of learners on my side when I say that that expectation is a case of misplaced function.

This is not all that we heard as we listened to these people in church settings, rural and urban and suburban, large and small. These are some of the major recurring themes. We also heard how people differ from one another in their learning patterns. Even the recurring themes are put together in unique patterns, person after person.

We heard learners talk about

- the influence of caring persons
- the significance of their early years
- how wise people shared wisdom
- the importance of involvement
- that consistency of presence helped learners in role modeling
- that the dailiness of life and other ordinary moments are motivators
- the way they learn in bursts as motivated by specific needs
- how adults and children and those in between continue in a lifelong pattern of learning by absorbing the enviroment
- a nostalgia for a time when learning was straight-forward and teaching seemed much more simple
- how important it is to be listened to in order to learn

As we heard people describe bits and pieces of their unique pattern, a list of more than eighty identifiable factors emerged as significant in describing learner behavior. We suspect that that list is only a beginning. If you will listen to the learners in your church, you will discover your own long list and your own themes.

The main purpose of this book is to encourage you to ask the people around you in the church how they learn. By discovering that local pattern, then, whatever your role, you will be able to respond to those around you with specific knowledge of learning patterns. We think that is a very good place to begin. Even, as we said above, when you rediscover the obvious, you will find it has life and power because it will be clothed in reality.

In the sections that follow we will address specific groups of people in order to suggest what may be the significance for them of these themes.

Listening is so basic to all this process that it deserves focused attention in response to the questions, How can I listen effectively to find out how people learn? and, How can I do more good listening in my teaching?

We learned another thing. I have saved it until this point to give it final emphasis. People *are* learning; they are learning in ways they enjoy, and they are open to learn more when the time is right. That is where the title of this book came from: We heard learning praised, and now we join in that affirmation of one of the quietly nice things in life. One said it very simply: "To me, learning is the most important thing you can get. . . . For me, learning is *the* important thing in life."

CHAPTER 3

To Teachers

Is the church-school teacher an endangered species? If there is any danger of that being true, I want to form a protective organization and save them from extinction. Probably we do not appreciate the enormous influence that good church-school teachers have had on many people.

Once upon a time, and only a generation ago for many, children could go to Sunday school and be sure of one thing—their teacher would be there. In the midst of the whirling, almost circus-like, impression that the whole church had on a child, there was one certain stable point, the teacher. Those who experienced that dependable relationship and that warmth and care look back now after many years of distance and remember those teachers. Comments such as:

Those Sunday school teachers were always patient. They were always there. You could depend on those people like clockwork. And it was just the fact that they were there that provided the example.

I always loved Sunday school and I can remember my church school teachers down home. . . . My church school teacher was very faithful and conscientious.

She was a good teacher, very faithful, and I happened to be in the town I grew up in when my daughter was in the first grade, and she had the same teacher for Sunday school.

I remember two church school teachers, neither of whom did it right, but they were there every Sunday, and you knew they would be there every Sunday and they sort of expected you to be there every Sunday too.

Today many churches solve the teacher recruitment problem by rotating teachers in and out. Unless done with extreme care, it appears that that pattern can undercut the dependable relationship that children and youth and adults desire.

Why are people reluctant to teach? There are many reasons given, but one underlying current is *apprehension*. In the first section of this book we mentioned the theme of nostalgia for simple teaching and learning. The hypothesis raised then was that we are in an awkward period of too much technological knowledge but lack of wisdom. The end result is that Christian education seems very difficult.

Is there some way we can avoid an improperly simplistic stance and still reclaim some of the ordinariness of teaching/learning? Many learners have rather plain expectations. They want to get to know someone so that they can ask some questions and get some answers and talk about how they live their lives. "The thing that made the class extremely worthwhile was I got a chance to ask questions that I had not heard anybody else ask before, and, always got answers to them."

One child said: "I like church school because they don't waste my time. I really learn about God and the Bible." Is that a very unusual child? I do not think so.

We found that many adults have a bashful sense of inadequacy concerning their knowledge of the Bible. They want to know some general basic facts about Bible content. Other adults see the church-school class as a place where they can find a Christian experience in human scale.

This was a place that I trusted. These were people and this was a place where I could feel comfortable and feel loved and affirmed and learn and then do some things that really made sense.

By that I mean they will be with few enough people long enough that they will have a sense of comfortable belonging.

We could wrestle with those plain expectations by asking, What do they really want? What are they really needing? My suggestion is that we take those statements at face value and begin there. Who knows how far we might be able to go with our teachers' agendas if we did a good job with the first steps, their first steps? Speaking from personal experience, an educator said, "I want to reemphasize that I'm not against planning education, but I really think we have to use the agenda that comes to us, and be intentional about that."

The items mentioned so far lead us back to the question, How can we reclaim some of the ordinariness of teaching and reduce some of the apprehension? Some of the simple expectations learners have of teaching are these: Teaching involves showing up. Teaching involves being dependable, trustworthy in routine things, willing to listen to the learner's agendas, willing to repeat basic truths over again, willing to work with learners so they can learn about God and the Bible.

Children said to us that they really did not want another day of school, but they did want to learn. Adults remembered their childhood experiences in the church school, and, beyond the memories of people already mentioned, they remembered a few basic global truths like "God is love" and "Jesus died for me" and "I should love others."

Children also told us quite often about the little play, the Christmas event when they sang, the day they received their Bibles. All these events I interpret as moments of heightened recognition when just enough challenge was combined with just enough success so that the children could feel they were important members of the church. That is one of their simple expectations.

Youth spoke too and said "You know." The pattern is like this:

It makes you realize some things about yourself, you know, hey, you know. Maybe I do need to improve on this or, you know, or say, hey, I'm like that or I didn't know that he was like that. Maybe I'm like that too, you know.

I recognize this to be a current speech habit, a way of punctuating oral conversation, but it strikes me as being a provocative habit. Youth do say and ask, "Do you know?" They want to know if anyone has been where they are and knows what it is like. They want a teacher who is some kind of bridge between the childhood they have not fully left and the adulthood they have not fully entered.

Youth spoke often of the importance of being significantly involved in some part of the life of the church as the way they learn. Youth, I think, need to begin teaching, probably in a supervised tutorial model so that they can learn and teach at the same time. Some will learn best through other significant leadership and servant roles.

And adult expectation? Adult motivation patterns require a variety of opportunities for learning. Informal learning through the environment continues to be important for adults. We need to find ways to respond to a sudden interest in a topic, and ways to relax our expectations so we are not over-programming (scheduling ten high-powered sessions when two guided conversations would be sufficient).

Adults need to be listened to, need to be heard. A layman in a church related:

> We were approached by a person and he said, "We're having some expriences in our life. . . . Isn't there a group in the church that I can come and sit down and talk over my problem and have somebody listen to me?"

Many times the only way an adult can find an attentive and trained listener is by reaching a crisis stage in faith or life. Adults are ready, however, to respond before a crisis situation arises and will learn in such a process. Some small-group models are a good step toward this kind of teaching, but some suffer from having no trained listener as part of the mix.

We can help teachers overcome their apprehension by affirming that what is most needed in any classroom is a loving, caring, and dependable person. To that can be added the skills and understandings that lead to increased effectiveness, but we should not place so much emphasis on technical aspects of teaching that we smother the human dimensions.

In the section directed to parents (and grandparents) I have elaborated on the role of the wise person. You can turn to that section so that a word-for-word repetition is not necessary here. Many of the learners we talked to paid tribute to someone who was that kind of person for them. Many times it was a church-school teacher. What some teachers do best, as far as learners are concerned, is share their considered opinions in terse, memorable stories and sayings.

Now, how should I phrase the lead-in to a conclusion? Should I say, "So you want to be a church-school teacher?" (hoping that what we have suggested so far has encouraged you to say "I can do that"); or should I say, "So you do not want to be a church-school teacher" (and try one more time to change your mind)? Maybe this will encourage people of both persuasions: learners are ordinary people; teachers should be ordinary too. Looking back, an adult said, "I'm thinking about three people that have had a lot to do with shaping my Christian living—just ordinary, plain people who had been touched by the Supreme Being."

The best quality you can bring to the class is credibility, and credibility means that the learners can recognize themselves in you. Are you ordinary enough to be a teacher?

I do not want to be misinterpreted as saying that teaching is not a challenging craft worthy of our best efforts in preparation. Teachers should be engaged in a constant refinement of their abilities to construct lesson plans and use creative approaches and understand the growth and development of the student. But all of this follows and is an addition to the simple and straight-forwardness being oneself. No technique is meant to replace persons and their natural and ordinary relation-ships.

In our mobile society, one loss we suffer is that of not being close enough to tell people how important they were to us (when we come to this realization down the pike). Some church-school teachers do not know they have been remembered and appreciated by one of those

learners in one of those classes some years ago. The
teacher gets discouraged.

You, dear teacher, are going to be remembered in a
humbling, appreciative way. You will be remembered for
being there, for caring, for being yourself, and for
teaching. Sometimes the "memory" will be immediate, as
in this instance:

> Roger was about two, and he just loved his teacher, Bob. And even
> after he was out of that class, and for a year afterward, he would just
> run up and hug Bob because he remembered him. I don't think
> people realize how much they are going to receive in return for
> teaching.

Sometimes it will be from the anonymous future, as this
adult said quietly, "I have a lot of memories of Sunday
school, all positive, and I know it had a strong influence
on my life." I am sorry you may not know that directly. I
hope this indirect and belated message reaches you,
really reaches you, down deep inside, and brings a warm
glow in your soul.

CHAPTER 4

To Learners

Words to the learner should begin with a message of appreciation and apology. You are, after all, what this is all about. It is what you, the learner, do that is the final realization of all other aspects of the education process. It has been your willingness to put shape and substance into the descriptions of your learning that has built this book.

In appreciation then, may I say that I have been greatly encouraged by the way in which you have persisted in gaining the knowledge that you have needed. I am impressed with the manner of your learning trek. I am grateful to know that you will approach learning, as you have previously approached it, with individuality of style.

The need for an apology is overdrawn. You seem to carry few grudges and voice few complaints. However, I do believe that those of us who have given direction to the education process have forgotten from time to time that it is your learning that is our objective. We have allowed ourselves to become short-circuited into running programs and managing schools and writing lessons and perfecting techniques. These are not bad except when they become ends instead of means. At our worst we have measured our success by compiling statistics and losing sight of that individuality mentioned above.

It may be that the following words of encouragement are not needed, but in case you have some reluctance to

enjoy your learning, I repeat them as gentle reminders of
your essential rights.

As we listened we heard you describe patterns of
learning that are spasmodic and utilitarian. "Curiosity was
always my motive for learning things back in school, but
now it's pure survival." Either of those descriptions might
be frowned upon. The frowns are uncalled for. It seems
quite legitimate for you to learn on the basis of your need
to know, and if that need is born out of moments of your
life that stand as disconnected islands, then so be it. If your
commitment of energy to learning is grounded on
immediate usefulness, then that is where it is grounded.

You have no need to be ashamed about setting your own
pace, developing your own agenda, and rating on your
own terms the resources and formats for learning. While
at times it may be necessary for you to adapt to the way
teachers know how to teach, most of the time, teachers and
systems should respond to your learning styles.

You have, in addition, the right to ask for solid
responses to your questions. The fact that you will make
up your own mind should not be used as an excuse to
always be "processed" and never be taught. I am convinced
that, with just a bit of guidance, you will assert your
strength in the learning/teaching dialogue. As you do so,
most teachers will find themselves freed to be active in
their own strength.

From time to time you talked to us with a note of
apology for not knowing something. I am sure you realize,
however, that those feelings of inadequacy are the
beginnings of learning and are not grounds for embar-
rassment. Bluffing, or avoiding a learning context because
you do not already know what you need to learn,

becomes absurd. Plunge in wherever the pond beckons, near the shore or in the depths. Get in over your head without apology. Follow the main lines or pursue the back roads. It is your journey!

I do not know quite what to make of it, but sometimes you seem to learn by remembering. It is not that you just remember, however; it is that you reshape those memories on the basis of the present and out comes something new. One learner described it this way. "It didn't seem like I learned much, but they keep coming back. I keep getting bits and pieces of it, it catches up and makes a lot of sense now." If you have not gone on a nostalgic journey through your own past, I would recommend it. We found people doing just that as they talked to us, and it was a time of learning.

I sense that we have had an implicit definition of learning which emphasizes the new. Do not we also learn what we already know? Do not we learn by calling back to consciousness the people and events and insights of the past to see how they fit the present? Learning is a process of elimination as well as accumulation. The nostalgic journey is a combination of recall and reinterpretation and letting go. One side effect we noticed was that people were surprised to find out how much they already knew.

One of the best ways to learn, if we take the many times it was mentioned as our guide, is to teach. That includes learning in order to have something to teach. It also means learning by the teaching itself. Just putting something you know out for others to share is transforming. The reactions of the learners add to this learning-by-teaching as well. In the words of a teacher:

> The thing that I enjoy most is teaching a class. For me that's one of the best ways to learn also, to actually get into the process

and study it so that I can teach it, and then in the teaching of it so
many other things come out.

If you find your learning getting stale, teach.

We could not begin to catalogue in a systematic way all
the places and resources you have told us about as you
described your learning. It is as if the whole world is your
curriculum packet. You pick up a piece here, add
something to it from over there, fill in the chinks with an
idea or a notion from way back then, click your fingers
and blink your eyes, and have the insight you are after.
The way you use this wide variety of resources is a skill to
be treasured.

About the Bible . . . It may be—one of us thought it
might be—that you mention wanting to know about the
Bible because that is a sort of obvious, acceptable thing to
say. On the other hand, and only you know the answer to
this, you may be identifying a persistent, real concern. I
can see why any Christian would want to have a better
grasp of our basic book. I can believe that even
well-schooled people may have a desire for a refresher
course in basics. What you have to insist upon, however,
is that you get what you want since there seems to be no
end to the people who know what you need to learn
without bothering to ask.

If there is one aspect of learning that I wish were more
evident, it is the step of focusing on what is to be learned
before the process takes off in full flight. Call it goal
setting or agenda-planning or getting down to brass tacks
or what you will, I think time spent on this pre-learning
step pays off. In travel we seldom set out on a journey
with no destination in mind. Even when the goal is
"exploration," we have said that to ourselves. In learning,
however, we often seem to plunge into a program with

little conscious planning of what we want to acquire. This lack of planning and failure to establish a learning goal undercuts motivation and makes evaluation very difficult.

Saying, "I want to learn more about the Bible" is more useful as a goal than saying "I want to learn something." It is even more helpful to think through that desire for Bible study another step in order to be able to say something like "I need a general review of the whole Bible" or "I want to compare the Gospels and the Epistles and see what differences I can recognize" or "I want to understand the concept of the kingdom of God as developed in the Gospel of Matthew."

As you know from the first and last sections of this book, listening is a major theme. You taught us this. You learn by being listened to, by being heard. The minor tragedy in our patterns of interaction is that you have picked up from somewhere that you have no right to be listened to with any expertise unless you are in the midst of great pain and turmoil. So, instead of being served in the education setting by good listeners dealing with the bits and pieces of ordinary learning, you are served by talkers. There should be both, and it is the listening that we ought to do something about. It can happen. After only a brief exercise in communication skills, a pastor reported,

> What can happen in the Christian community of faith is for persons willing to share their own backgrounds, and others, who have different backgrounds, to listen and see if they can't grow through their shared experiences. . . . I know that sometimes it is kind of hard, because I guess we fear most the unknown.

Your role in this can be to be more aggressive in securing the time and space and persons that let you learn by being heard. The training of listeners is going to take some time, but nothing will happen if you do not persist.

I did not conjure up the title of this book just to catch your attention. The title reflects what I found out in the hours of interviewing that we did. Learners *are* praising learning. You are learning. You are happy about learning. You have an openness to more learning. Learning is alive and well because you, the learners, are alive and well (and holding forth in every nook and cranny of the church).

CHAPTER 5

To Parents and Grandparents

To Parents

> I began to realize that a lot of things that I learned growing up in my family life influence me now. I can only recognize these looking back as instruments of God's grace. My mother and my father are probably the most significant people that influenced my life.

Parents, you are still a very critical factor in the education of your children. For some of you that is good news, and for others it is bad news.

If you want to help your children appreciate and understand the Christian faith, if you hope that they will find that faith important as you have, if you are concerned about the development of their ethical and religious life with a commitment similar to that which many parents devote to the nurture of intellectual and physical ability, then the news from children, from adults who recall their childhood, from teachers and educators, is that you *are* important. The news is good. Again and again someone would echo this thought: "Well, my parents had a very great influence on my life. My mother was always very active in church and always believed very much in the mission of the church and being in mission beyond just Sunday morning."

Some parents feel that their children have been taken

away from them by the flood of agencies and programs
that characterize our society. So much is this the case that
some parents feel their role has been reduced to doing
the laundry, cooking some of the meals, and providing
transportation to the next event. In the midst of that
competition for the attention of the child the good news
is that parents still have an open door to influence the
child's faith.

On the other hand, if you want somebody else to take
over the task of religious nurture, if you really would like
to have this area of their development as your neutral
territory, if you are so confused by the flux in religious
ideas and fads that you want to throw up your hands and
say, "Go ask somebody else," the news is not encouraging. The news is bad. You are still important.

On the basis of our interviews this seems to be the way
it works, this relationship between parent and child in
religious matters:

1) Children sense, long before they have the ability to
understand the patterns objectively, whether or not the
church is important to the parent(s). They start off with a
value bias that is intuitive. A parent said, "I've learned
that my children pick up a lot more than I wish they did
from the way I live, and a lot less from the way I want to
live. They are very impressionable."

2) Children read behavior, that is, they know whether
or not the parent participates with consistency in the life
of the church. They know whether or not they are *sent* to
church or *accompanied*. On the basis of this reading of
behavior they conclude how important those matters
related to church are to the parents(s). Memories of her
childhood have influenced this woman who said, "I
wished then that my parents went like other parents did.
Maybe that's why we hardly ever miss church with our

children. Maybe it's because I feel I missed out as a child."

3) Children listen. They do not listen for a systematic theology. They do not listen for a complete recital of biblical history. They listen for the occurrence of God language in reference to the problems of their lives. Does God relate to their fears? Is God seen as concerned about their problems? Is God dependable? Listen to this child. "If you're scared you don't need to be scared 'cause God is always with us.' [Who told you that?] My dad. My dad tells me lots of things about God."

4) Children remember. They remember global statements. They remember them because they believe them. They believe them because parent(s) believe them. When they press for answers in those long chains of "why" and "how," they seem to be pressing for assurance rather than explanation. "Do you really believe that?" is the functional significance of the "why" and the "how." And as the parent explains, the message is the reassurance, "Yes. I believe this, and you can too."

5) Children are looking for a consistency of presence. They want someone who will give them honest answers to their questions, even honest admissions of "I don't know," but they want to be able to ask the question. Someone must be there, in their lives, in an open and dependable fashion. They need explanations of the decisions of life. A parent talked about a changing pattern in his family and gave this advice:

> We should talk about moral values. We assume that they're taught without talking, and I don't believe that's really true. If I get too much change from the store, what should I do? Should I give it back or not? And if I should, why should I? With the first child we talked about it, and then when the other three came along we still gave the change back, but we never said anything about it. In our day and age I'm not sure children always understand the things you do.

6) If matters of faith are important to the parents, then children move rather freely and easily through the whole of life and the whole of the church putting together adequate insights for living. They construct their own systems of interpretations, sufficient for the time being, and proceed with the business of living at hand.

The role of the parents in the teaching of their children is indicated in this too simple but essentially common reflection of the views of our learners. Some children learn in spite of their parents. They happen into relationships with other adults; the words we have for teachers in another section, and to grandparents later on in this section, are based on that possibility. The surer bet, however, is that children will reflect the basic faith stance of their parents and move into the acquisition of more precise knowledge of the faith, with a bias for or against that stems from parental roots.

Parents are not excused from having that influence just because they have some gaps in their knowledge in matters of faith. It is not the content that children use as the criteria of importance. It is the attitude they adopt, and they pick up the attitude from ordinary and repeated parent behavior. One inactive member sent her daughter to church in her place. My guess is that the child understands that she is going in her mother's place and knows that she is expected to take the church more seriously than her mother does. My guess is that she probably will not.

The patterns of religious life in the home among those we talked to were quite varied. Some had specific religious moments of Bible reading and/or prayer. Others had a much more casual pattern of saying grace at meals and infrequent discussions of religious matters. A

teen-ager describes one such pattern in response to the
question, Who influences your faith?

> My dad, because we've just done so many things together. We have
> our talks together. In your early teens you think you know it all and
> you don't go by your parent's reasoning too much. But then you get
> older and tend to realize that maybe, Hey, my parents have
> something there. Maybe they know what they're talking about.

It did not appear that the pattern of specifically religious
moments was as critical as the sensed importance of
matters of faith in the whole parental life-style.

Participation in the life of the institutional church was
a major factor in our interviews. One recollection was
stated this way:

> Well, it started from the home. . . . My mother was religious and my
> father, they were both members of the church and the church
> school. See, if you have parents that are in the church there's
> nothing left for you to do but also be in the church.

In an age when the institutional form of the Christian
faith has been discounted by many, that pattern seems to
be a significant warning. Children told us that the church
was important to them. Church school and worship and
choir and drama and fellowship hour and potluck
supper all floated in and out of their conversations as
clues to the meaning of Christianity. Parents remain the
key to that institutional reality for children. Thus parents
must see squarely the great difficulty they face when they
imagine they can avoid the church and still affirm
Christianity among children who need concrete expres-
sions of faith.

It is not uncommon to find adults who are a bit uncertain of their ability to represent adequately Christianity for children. It is the same anxiety that makes it difficult to recruit teachers. Parents are not immune to this lack of confidence in religious matters. The compensating force is that, for children, the process of learning about matters of faith is as natural as the process of learning how to talk and how to read and how to live. Parents are not expected to be highly sopisticated religious technicians with computer-like recall of theological and biblical data shaped by an accurate familiarity with plans of intellectual and moral and faith development.

No, the expectation of parents is that they will communicate to their children by behavior and word the core realities of their faith, day in and day out, in the normal process of living. Children do not expect perfection nearly as much as they expect dependability. Then parents, and others, become the influence described by one this way: "It was Sunday school teachers, my dad and my mother, people I was around. People that I looked up to and really truly knew they were good people. They're the ones that really touched me."

Parents have a responsibility in faith matters that is very much like the responsibility they accept in music education. If you will, pretend that helping your child learn Christianity is like helping that child learn to play the piano. In both, when you sense a level of readiness, you encourage the child, find a good teacher, expect the child to go to the lesson times regularly, and practice in between. The parent may or may not be a pianist. The parent may or may not, even if a pianist, be able to conduct the formal teaching of his or her own child. But neither of those conditions prevents many parents from introducing their children to music, to musical talent, to training in playing the piano. Christianity deserves that kind of parental concern and similar parental action.

The word we heard on parents is not only one of importance, but also one of possibility. Parents of all sorts have had a strong positive influence on the faith of their children. We did hear that some people did not become conscious of that influence until years later. The parent may not have the blessing of immediate clear appreciation. It may be a good idea for discouraged parents to sit down and listen to some adults as they reflect back over the years so they can see how important the small things they are doing now may be when the picture is painted by their children years hence.

To Grandparents

One of the most fascinating themes in the descriptions of learning that we heard was the role of the grandparent. It was not always the bloodline grandparent—it could be a grandparent figure—but time and again people recalled the influence of such a person on their faith in the childhood years. We heard many comments like these:

> What I learned, I learned from my grandmother and from attending church and the Sunday school people.

> My grandmother and my grandfather. My grandfather was, I would say, more religious even than my grandmother.

We puzzle over this theme. Why were grandparents and their counterparts mentioned so often? Is that pattern going on today, or were we seeing a pattern of extended family life that has been destroyed in our splintered life-styles? What is it that the grandparent does that the parent and teacher seemingly cannot do? We do not have the answers to those queries, but we do have some suggestions.

The grandparent has a relationship with a child that is one of closeness and yet distance. That means that grandparents function as wise people for children. Grandparents have the freedom to be frank and simple in matters of faith that others find difficult because of too many other important relational agendas. A child can get to know the grandparent over a number of years in a variety of settings, in contrast to the much more restricted pattern of the teacher-child and the much more complicated relationship of parent-child.

When this pattern of relationships is combined with the freedom some grandparents have to reduce life to its simplest elements, the stage is set for a unique pattern of influence. At least that is our speculation. You can test this out in your own reflections on life and in conversations with other learners.

The "so what" for today is that while children still could find a "grandparent" relationship of great importance in learning the faith, where are the grandparents? How can we facilitate this relationship for children? Grandparents, where are you? Are you hiding? Have you been away from children so long that they frighten you? Have you become convinced that only the young understand life and that you have no wisdom to share? Wherever you are, and whatever you feel, know this: children need you!

Children need your presence in their lives over some years. Children need you to tell them the story of your life. Children need to hear your bits of wisdom. Children need to hear you recite the biblical stories. Children need your sense of history, your perspective, your love. A church-school teacher said, "There is a lack of elderly people participating in our Sunday school, and I don't think they realize how much they can give to the children. I know they had a big influence on my life."

The parent's responsibility in this is to find each child a grandparent. Parents, more than anyone else, can help create the long-term relationship with the person of wisdom who can be a great influence on the faith development of the child. Of course, the dynamic is not fully described in these few paragraphs, but you get the idea.

Intergenerational learning events in a church can foster the child-grandparent relationship. So can the way you begin to be involved in your neighborhood. I think, however, that new steps toward the encouragement of this phase of learning will have to involve your home and family life to be effective.

Good news, bad news, parents and grandparents are very important in the religious and faith growth of children. Challenge and comfort? Few adults feel so competent that they have no sense of inadequacy in this task. Yet, time and again we heard how effective ordinary parents and grandparents have been in communicating that basic sense of importance and encapsulated wisdom to their children. If they can, you can.

CHAPTER 6

To Pastors, Educators, and Other Leaders

Watch an accomplished gymnast—all the movements appear effortless. Watch a novice—the same movements are strenuous. The difference is that the accomplished gymnast has learned to perform only those body actions which produce the desired result, while much that the novice is doing is counterproductive.

The analogy serves to point the direction for the kind of leadership that is needed to enhance learning: When leadership is appropriate to the essential needs of learners it may have all the appearance of being effortless. Do not be deceived, however, and conclude that no leadership is the best leadership. On the other hand, a wild flurry of programming, a constant search for innovation, can consume so much energy from everyone that learning is rendered difficult and complicated, nigh onto impossible.

The task of leaders is to know the situation well enough to know what essential guidance is needed so that the very natural process of learning can take place. One critical step in the pursuit of that awareness is the simple, yet often neglected, on-site research into learning. How often have we raced ahead without asking learners in our context how they learn!

In the process of our conversations with learners we found a considerable variety of patterns. Learning is a complex set of social interactions shaped by the unique histories, interests, and needs of individuals. Yet we found some patterns. Those patterns constitute a promise rather than a prescription. If you will listen carefully to those in your setting, you will find a similar combination of the unique and the common. Furthermore, you will find that concepts you are familiar with as theory, come alive in provocative concreteness.

In church after church, leaders in education have conducted interest surveys. Those just will not be adequate. To be sure, such a procedure is better than blind programming, but not much. People are not used to being asked how they learn. When asked to comment on the interview experience, one person said:

> It's been a good opportunity to say some things. . . . It's one thing to hide behind a cloak of idealism. It's another thing to look at the cold, hard reality of things and hopefully learn from both. We should keep our high ideals, but we have to work with what is real, and then try to blend and mix, influence, and mold something better than what we've got.

The process takes more attentive listening than a form provides. With attentive listening, learners can discover and verbalize their styles. In the process they will also begin to discover interests and needs that are of a different quality than rating items on an interest menu.

Leaders, take the time to listen, and I think you will be helped to see what you can do to enhance learning. You must, however, be willing to hear what the learners are saying (in contrast to hearing what you want them to say). Hearing requires being willing to start where learners want to start. It requires holding back from imposing our "better" learning agendas. The temptation to assume that one knows what others need to know better than they do seems to be an unfortunate side effect of training for leadership in education. Another of the side effects is the assumption that education is the cure-all for all ills. As an educator I find myself being asked to assume the "savior" role for any aspect of church life that is not what it is supposed to be. If the people of the church do not give enough, if they do not work hard enough, if they do not worship frequently enough, if they are not good enough parents, if they do not support the evangelism program or the social action program vigorously enough, it is always because they do not know enough. Create an education program and the other problem will be solved.

That messianic understanding of education is a convenient misplacement of responsibility. Learning can affect people in all the areas mentioned, but that does not justify placing on education the cure-all responsibility. The overload of expectation on education diverts attention from other reasons for the existence of those problems and prevents education from carrying out its legitimate serving role in the lives of people and institutions. Ironically, letting learning proceed on a less grandiose path frees it to be more effective in the course of growth.

Another unfortunate side effect of training in leadership is that through an increased awareness of the technical dimensions of teaching/learning, we become servants of the technology instead of servants of learners. Technique is not only a matter of developing a repertoire of skills and a file cabinet full of resources. It is also a matter of becoming committed to an unnatural language system of jargon. The result of this increased technical sophistication is, unfortunately, the sidetracking of education leaders into technician roles that fall short when measured by the ruler of common sense.

I am *not* advocating a naïve and simplistic approach to education. I *am* advocating going beyond the technician level to the simplicity imaged in the analogy of the accomplished gymnast. Learners, for example, if we will ask them and listen to what they say, will tell us how they learn, what motivates their learning, what kinds of resources they use, and what patterns of relationships are genuinely helpful. If we will hear them, start wherever they want to start, and serve them well at that level, the door to all that we might hunger for stands open.

Listening is a task for leaders as a process of teaching, besides being a step in preparation for learning. I think the burden for providing trained listeners and occasions for listening falls most fully on education leaders. It is our task to acquire these skills and sensitiveness ourselves. Then it is our task to train others. The importance of this theme in our research has led us to pay fuller attention to the rationale and process of listening in the final section of this book. The possibility was attained in one church as the pastor reported:

> They've been shaking hands with people and sharing a few things like you do during the Ritual of Friendship in the pew, but in this instance they were sitting down and asking something and listening to the response and all of a sudden these people are talking to each other and listening to each other.

All too often education leaders find themselves in an administrative position to the exclusion of teaching. I think that must change. The leaders and their supportive institutions must both change their perceptions to include teaching as a central role. The nonteaching pastor, educator, or volunteer leader should be the exception rather than the rule. Preaching is not a

sufficient substitute for teaching in most instances.
Making education decisions (or guiding boards and
committees as they make those decisions) when one has no
regular relationship with learners in a teaching/learning
situation cuts one off from the groundsprings of the entire
enterprise. Learners are what it is all about. I am aware
that schooling serves the church in many nonlearning
ways. Groups and classes provide a human-scale arena
within the institution and promote a sense of belonging.
Classes often minister to their members in providing care
and support in the midst of the joys and pains of life. Given
all those values for schooling, the point remains that the
primary objective of education is learning, and adminis-
trators ought to keep themselves in the teaching/learning
relationship.

Leaders have the opportunity, and thus the responsibility, to assume the advocacy role for learners in the life
of the whole church. Let us repeat some cliches: The
whole church teaches; people of all ages learn from all
that the church does. Our learners supported those
well-known statements again and again. Most of the time
they were *not* experiencing internal conflict as they
exprienced the whole church and learned from all that
the church does. Still it would not hurt for leaders in
education to "walk through" the life of the church with a
particular learner in mind and ask of everything they see,
What does this teach?

Children are particularly vulnerable in this way. As the
fourth-graders we talked to described their experience
of the church, we received a picture of a whirling mass of
perceptions more like a three-ring circus than anything
else. In answering, What do you learn in church? a child
went through this almost painful description:

Well, you learn the Bible and sometimes you learn new stuff, well. If you don't know it and like that and then there's other stuff like if you want to know, let's see, like how to be more religious and stuff like that and then, that's about it.

That is not surprising, given the nature of the child. But the child is caught in that maelstrom with very little power to do anything about it, other than experience it, come what may. And what do they experience? Something as inconspicuous as this, in reply to "What's your favorite place in the church?" "My favorite place is the drinking fountain when I get thirsty."

I know that there are those of some theological persuasions who firmly believe that children have no rights. I know that our society shows signs of being less and less inclined to give children a fair shake in general education. I know that some are so intent on securing an adult conversion from children that they treat children as little adults and turn everything that might be education into indoctrination for decision. I deplore all of that and appeal for education leaders to see as part of their task the monitoring of the whole life of the church as advocates for children.

Leaders in education must also take seriously the relationship between consistency, ritual, participation, and learning. We noted that children have a strong appreciation for that teacher who "is always there." Others spoke of the importance to them of learning through participation in the ritual acts of worship. In part, people learn through the symbolic truths which are always somewhat beyond definition, but in a less profound sense, people also learn from dependable repetitions of presence and action. The education strategy which emphasizes the new, to the exclusion of the dependably familiar, undercuts this aspect of learning.

In the area of sales there is a tendency for those doing the selling to become bored with their dependable presentation. For their own interest they begin to alter that presentation for the sake of novelty. I suspect that those in the pastoral ministry may suffer from a similar "presentation fatigue" and seek forms of expression that are new for the sake of newness. But people use global statements of truth as handles for entire systems of meaning and sets of entire relationships. If we realize this, then we can provide the repetitions of these affirmations to the extent that they are needed by the learners. The best-known verse in the Bible rings true to this fourth-grade girl:

> The best part of it is when he says, "Whosoever believeth in me shall not perish, but have everlasting life," because that means a lot to me because if you don't love God then you'll perish, but if you love him a lot then you'll always have life with God. [What does "perish" mean?] I'm not sure, but I get the meaning when I hear it.

In the first section we suggested that those who pick up this book can find the section which addresses their situation or role most closely and read that first. They may not want to read any other section. The exception to that advice is for those in leadership roles. You are urged to begin to familiarize yourself with the perspective of others by reading the sections addressed to them. You are strongly urged to read the section on listening, for the reasons mentioned above. Both serve as steps toward the final urging, that you explore your own context in a careful and attentive manner.

What will result from that on-site research is learning. You will learn where the children, youth, and adults are in your context. Thus you will have that specific and concrete base on which to provide leadership in the decision-making process related to education.

You have fully as much right to learn in your own style as does anyone else. Identify your own learning patterns as you explore the patterns of others. See clearly your strongest pattern and plan your own growth and development accordingly. In doing so you will provide a model for learning that will encourage others to stand in their strength and become co-learners in the journey of faith.

CHAPTER 7

To Children

I am dividing this section into two parts. In the first part, I have some words of warning. In the second part, I have some words of hope.

Words of Warning

I am sorry to report that the world you live in is not always glad to see you. Some adults are afraid of you. They are afraid that you are going to get in their way. They are afraid that you are going to take up too much of their time. They are afraid that it is going to cost too much to raise you.

The adults who are afraid of you are going to avoid you if they can. You will find places that are marked off "For Adults Only," and you will not be wanted in those places. You will find some adults who will send you away in order to avoid spending time with you. You will find some adults who will never really listen to you because they do not want to hear what you say.

If possible, you should not feel that you are responsible for the fears adults have of you and of other children. Even when those adults try to make you feel bad because *they* are afraid, you should try to remember (somewhere deep inside your own thoughts) that you are not the

CHAPTER 8

On Listening

We listened with the desire to find out how people learn. They expressed appreciation for our listening and described it as a learning experience. The intensity with which they said this prompts us to say three things:

1. The process of listening to learners is an extremely valuable way to establish relevance in education programming.
2. Attentive listening is a valuable teaching process.
3. Training listeners should be one of the first leadership development objectives for the church.

Listening has a firmly established place in counseling. Being able to hear what the counselee says is a prerequisite of all that follows. Many times the listening process is most of what is needed, and the counselee leaves the process with the pain and the problem under control.

Listening has a firmly established value in prayer and meditation. The quieting of one's being so that the still small voice may speak is known to be essential to cultivating an awareness of the Almighty. We pray, and in our speaking and listening, claim a God who also both listens and speaks. To be able to listen is to take on the quality of godliness.

Many people, when they stop to think about it, have no difficulty describing moments when the attentive listening of another has been a significant learning moment. And yet, with all these recommendations, we continue to identify teaching with talking or with a busyness of activities that makes steady and productive conversation almost impossible. Why this aversion?

Someone said it is a characteristic of the citizens of our country that our conversations are much more like golf than tennis. Each of us puts into play our own idea or feeling and then, with only a polite bow to others, we proceed to hit that ball from the first tee to the last green—on and on and on. In contrast, in tennis, two or more people work with one idea or feeling, and by necessity as well as choice must receive as well as return.

Perhaps our aversion is that we are "pre-minded"— that is, we already know what is going to be said, so we do not need to listen. We have heard it all before. People seldom come up with anything new. If they do not say what we want, we pretend that they do. We listen, but only for the momentary pause that allows us to break in on the pattern and speak. Perhaps we avoid listening because we have no real interest in anyone but ourselves.

It may be that listening is difficult because it involves us in change. If we really hear what is being said, we may have to respond in a manner that disrupts our lives. Thus it is better to listen very selectively, in order never even to hear that which might disturb our opinions, our plans, our privacy.

Listening may be avoided because it can be hard work. To listen—really listen—one must be able to concentrate, to accept the speaker, to be unfailingly honest and transparently real, and be willing to enter an experience from which the listener may not return unchanged. It can, in fact, as Douglas V. Steere said in his *Listening to Another*, be a personal ordeal.

Listening is not "just listening," nor is it indifference, nor is it what you do when you cannot think of what to say, nor is it all that there is to teaching. What it is, is a process of learning that can bring genuine insights to educators and is highly valued among learners.

It may be that we do not listen because we do not know how. Listening is a skill. It seems hardly ever to be one that is taught with any focused attention. We have (or used to have) courses in public speaking, but very seldom have I heard of anyone offering even a session on attentive listening. What might such an experience look like?

I think that persons who want to learn to listen must face some of the barriers and challenges to listening that we have already mentioned. Some of these seem rather trivial. I think they are not. Particularly, they are not inconsequential when they have become embedded in our lives as habits.

On the other side, I think we must begin to see the values of listening carefully. By listening we can develop insight into actual people. Too often we are at some distance from people as we relate in a pattern of mutual stereotypes. I find a label for you, and you find a category for me; I relate to the label, and you relate to the category. Listening is the means for breaking through these barriers to the realities of people.

Listening gives concreteness to the theoretical. Much of what learners told us about themselves, the themes of this book, is part of the theory of education. Beyond theory, however, are the concrete embodiments of those same truths. Those people bring the generalities to life with sound and color and clever twists and detail and story. Listening is the means to give life to what is already known.

Listening allows us to perceive the uniqueness that is the other person. Yes, the other person is real, and he or she brings life to theory, and comes alive as no other person on the face of the earth. Two people saying the same thing, word for word, do not say the same things. Finding those subtle differences by careful listening is exciting.

The picture that some paint for research is like the drilling of shallow test holes all over a landscape. Another form of research takes what time and other resources are available and goes much deeper, with fewer exploratory wells. Listening leads to depth understandings as the attentive ear allows the speaker to find the unknown in himself.

To these values of listening and to the challenges to listening we must then add a training process. Essentially, such training would involve practice sessions in which a time of listening is followed by the listener's reporting what has been said. Then, in one way or another (by reviewing the audio or video tape or having a reply from the speaker or getting the opinion of an impartial evaluator), the listener is helped to see how well the listening has gone. Then the cycle is repeated.

The practice sessions should be focused, and they are better when short in length to begin with. The listener should be encouraged to listen to *whole* people. That means to listen not only to the content of what is being said, but to all the other message carriers, such as tone of voice, body expression, and the significant silence. Listeners should be helped to slow down and stay in the here and now and not rush ahead into interpretation.

In our research process we did these things:

1) We asked for a full hour with each person. That seemed to be a good average length of time. People will

work with considerable effort for an hour. Beyond that, energy limits are reached.

2) We stated our desire to hear them tell us how they learn. The topic was usually mystifying, at first. We would often suggest that they describe their formal learning experiences, as an easy place to begin.

3) When they mentioned what seemed to be an important event or experience, we would ask them to describe at least part of that in as great detail as they could. We emphasized description, rather than evaluation. When opinions were offered, we accepted them, but tried to come back around to their learning picture as soon as we could.

4) We would provide a stimulus question when we had to (like inquiring about people and places and resources), but we tried to avoid a verbalized checklist.

5) We tried to be responsive to their portraits of learning, asking for greater detail and clarity by following their lead. Since we wanted to review the conversations at length, we taped all of them and had them transcribed. The on-site explorations you may conduct would not require that process, although listening to a taped playback adds greatly to the listener's insight.

The incorporation of listening into the teaching process in the classroom or formal setting has been most fully realized by the small group discussions that continue to be valuable to adult learners. The small group discussion at least provides the opportunity for more people to take part in the conversation. It is not guaranteed, however, that the increased participation will provoke attentive listening. The introduction of a trained listener into that process could enrich it.

To make listening possible the pace of teaching/learning must be controlled through a reduced student/teacher ratio and an uncrowded agenda. "More" in teaching is not always best, and in this instance "less" is more efficient. The time spent in listening serves the learners by allowing for their movement from the acceptable answer to the answer that is truly their own. When they have this alive-space that the careful listeners provide, they are encouraged to find their way through the unexplored dimensions of their own minds and discover the more basic issues, the more central affirmations, the deeper motivations.

We listened. You can too. I hope you will. I hope you will take these few guides and embark on your own research to guide the decision-making process of church education. I hope you will incorporate listening into the best of your other teaching skills. I hope you will urge upon the church the training of listeners for the enrichment of education. The learners are ready. They ask to be heard.

It may well be that the future of education lies not in our management of the new technology of education, nor in massive modifications of structures or curriculum, but in the understanding of the reason for all of this—the learner.